Phonics Celebration CD

Lyrics & Coloring Book

PHONICS CELEBRATION

The New Generation of Alphabet Songs, Chants and Phonics Fun!

Learn to Read Through Songs and Chants

"L.E.A.P. into your future"

The New Generation of Alphabet Songs, Chants, and Phonics Fun!

Marie Olga Alexandre

ISBN: 978-0-9975160-3-6

Printed in the United States of America

First Edition

To Lilia

Phonics Celebration
Lyrics
&
Coloring Book

Phonics Celebration
Music CD

Contents

Credits

Voice Actors/Actresses:

Erick Alexandre, Erole Alexandre,
Gerardson Alexandre, M.O. Alexandre,
Carline Antoine, Emily Aristilde,
Gregory Aristilde, Xavier Brown,
Sophie Charles, Guerlens Desir,
Berlynn Eustache, Jackson Lubke,
Frank Pagliaro, Gina Rodriguez,
Richard Saber, Taina Salony,
Tassaina Salony, Lilia Turenne,
Maggie Val, Nelson Val

Singers:

Gerardson Alexandre, M.O. Alexandre,
Emily Aristilde, Carline Antoine,
Daphney Charles, Sophie Charles,
Guerlens Desir, Berlynn Eustache,
Taina Salony, Tassaina Salony, Kesline Tilus,
Maggie Val

Musicians:
Pianists: Guerlens Desir, Daniel Laport
Guitarists: Despeignes Atis
Saxophonist: Nelson Val

Songwriter:
Marie Olga Alexandre

Sounds Engineer:
Daniel Laport

ABC CHANT REMIX

Featured voice actresses/singers: Carline Antoine, Sophie Charles, Taina Salony, Tassaina Salony

Directions: Track the lyrics with your finger as you sing along. Color the images.

Come along and chant with me.
(3 times)
It's an ABC chant.
Many of my friends
have chanted with me.
It's an ABC chant.

A	(clap clap clap clap)
B	(clap clap clap clap)
C D E	(clap clap clap clap)

F	(clap clap clap clap)
G	(clap clap clap clap)
H I J	(clap clap clap clap)

K	(clap clap clap clap)
L	(clap clap clap clap)
MNO	(clap clap clap clap)

P	(clap clap clap clap)
Q	(clap clap clap clap)

A Antelope	B Bear	
C Camel	D Deer	E Elephant
F Fox	G Giraffe	
H Horse	I Iguana	J Jaguar
K Kangaroo	L Lion	
M Mouse	N Nightingale	O Orangutan
P Pig	Q Quail	

ABC CHANT REMIX

R S T   (clap clap clap clap)

U   (clap clap clap clap)
V   (clap clap clap clap)

W X Y   (clap clap clap clap)

ZZZZZZZZZZZZZZZ

R — Rabbit	S — Sheep	T — Tiger
U — Unicorn	V — Vulture	
W — Whale	X — Xrayfish	Y — Yak
	Z — Zebra	

Come along and chant with me. (2 times)
It's an ABC chant.
Many of my friends have chanted with me.
It's an ABC chant.

Directions: *Track* the lyrics with your finger as you sing along. *Color* the images.

It's an ABC chant; come chant with me.
It's an ABC chant ..... my ABC's.

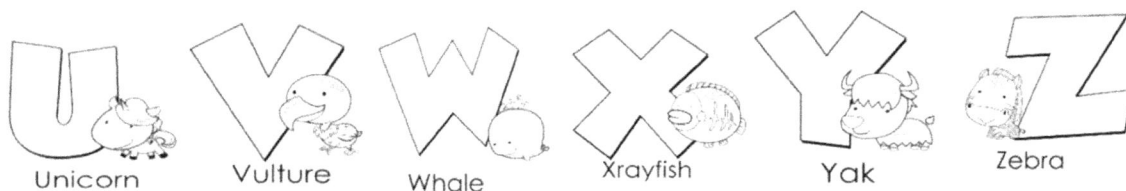

Antelope   Bear   Camel   Deer   Elephant

Fox   Giraffe   Horse   Iguana   Jaguar

It's an ABC chant; come chant with me.
It's an ABC chant ..... my ABC's.

Kangaroo   Lion   Mouse   Nightingale   Orangutan

Pig   Quail   Rabbit   Sheep   Tiger

It's an ABC chant; come chant with me.
It's an ABC chant ..... my ABC's.

Unicorn   Vulture   Whale   Xrayfish   Yak   Zebra

3

THE ALPHABET STORIES

Featured voice actresses/actors/singers: Erick Alexandre, Erole Alexandre, Gerardson Alexandre, M. O. Alexandre, Carline Antoine, Emily Aristilde, Gregory Aristilde, Sophie Charles, Guerlens Desir, Jackson Lubke, Gina Rodriguez, Richard Saber, Taina Salony, Tassaina Salony, Kesline Tilus, Maggie Val, Nelson Val

Directions: Track the lyrics with your finger as you sing along.
Color the images.

We all have a story; we all have a story;
we all have a story.
A has a story; (Tell us!). A has a story; (Tell us!).
A has a story and it makes 2 sounds.
A is my name (ā-ā). A is my name (ă-ă).
A is my name and I make 2 sounds.

/ā-ā-ā/→ acorn
/ă-ă-ă/ → apple
I make 2 sounds.

B has a story; (Tell us!). B has a story; (Tell us!).
B has a story and it makes 1 sound.
B is my name /b-b/. B is my name /b-b/.
B is my name and I make 1 sound.

/b-b-b /→ boy
/b-b-b/ → book
I make 1 sound.

C has a story; (Tell us!). C has a story, (Tell us!).
C has a story and it makes 2 sounds.
C is my name /k-k/. C is my name /s-s/.
C is my name and I make 2 sounds.

/k-k-k/ → cat
/s-s-s/ → cent
I make 2 sounds.

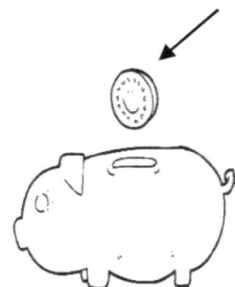

THE ALPHABET STORIES

D has a story; (Tell us!). D has a story, (tell us!).
D has a story and it makes 1 sound.
D is my name (d-d). D is my name (d-d).
D is my name and I make 1 sound.

d-d-d → dog
d-d-d → door
I make 1 sound.

E has a story, (tell us!). E has a story, (tell us!).
E has a story and it makes 2 sounds.
E is my name (ē-ē). E is my name (ĕ-ĕ).
E is my name and I make 2 sounds.

ē-ē-ē → eagle
ĕ-ĕ-ĕ → elephant
I make 2 sounds.

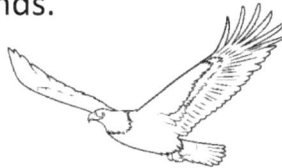

The Stories of FGHIJ

We all have a story; we all have a story;
we all have a story.
F has a story, (tell us!). F has a story, (tell us!).
F has a story and it makes 1 sound.
F is my name (f-f). F is my name (f-f).
F is my name and I make 1 sound.

f-f-f → fish
f-f-f → fig
I make 1 sound.

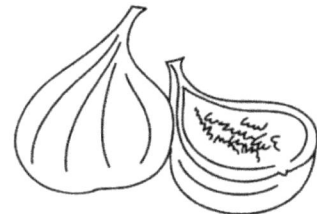

THE ALPHABET STORIES

G has a story, (tell us!). G has a story, (tell us!).
G has a story and it makes 2 sounds.
G is my name (g-g). G is my name (j-j).
G is my name and I make 2 sounds.

g-g-g → goat
j-j-j → giraffe
I make 2 sounds.

H has a story, (tell us!). H has a story; (tell us!).
H has a story and it makes 1 sound.
H is my name (h-h). H is my name (h-h).
H is my name and I make 1 sound.

h-h-h → hat
h-h-h → horse
I make 1 sound.

I has a story; (tell us!). I has a story; (tell us!).
I has a story and it makes 2 sounds.
I is my name (ī-ī). I is my name (ĭ-ĭ).
I is my name and I make 2 sounds.

ī-ī-ī → ice
ĭ-ĭ-ĭ → igloo
I make 2 sounds.

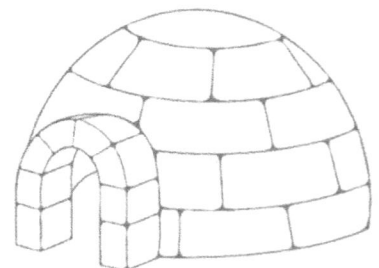

THE ALPHABET STORIES

J has a story, (tell us!). J has a story, (tell us!).
J has a story and it makes 1 sound.
J is my name (j-j). J is my name (j-j).
J is my name and I make 1 sound.

j-j-j → jump
j-j-j → jug
I make 1 sound.

The Stories of KLMNO

We all have a story; we all have a story;
we all have a story.
K has a story, (tell us!). K has a story, (tell us!).
K has a story and it makes 1 sound.
K is my name (k-k). K is my name (k-k).
K is my name and I make 1 sound.

k-k-k → kangaroo
k-k-k → kite
I make 1 sound.

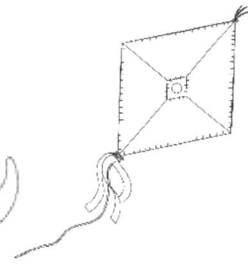

L has a story, (tell us!). L has a story, (tell us!).
L has a story and it makes 1 sound.
L is my name (l-l). L is my name (l-l).
L is my name and I make 1 sound.

l-l-l → lion
l-l-l → leg
I make 1 sound.

THE ALPHABET STORIES

M has a story, (tell us!). M has a story, (tell us!).
M has a story and it makes 1 sound.
M is my name (m-m). M is my name (m-m).
M is my name and I make 1 sound.

m-m-m → monkey
m-m-m → mouse
I make 1 sound.

N has a story, (tell us!). N has a story, (tell us!).
N has a story and it makes 1 sound.
N is my name (n-n). N is my name (n-n).
N is my name and I make 1 sound.

n-n-n → nose
n-n-n → neck
I make 1 sound.

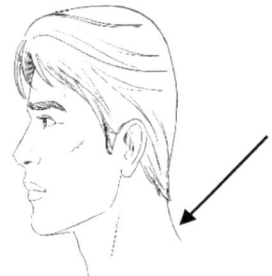

O has a story, (tell us!). O has a story, (tell us!).
O has a story and it makes 2 sounds.
O is my name (ō-ō). O is my name (ŏ-ŏ).
O is my name and I make 2 sounds.

ō-ō-ō → ocean
ŏ-ŏ-ŏ → octopus
I make 2 sounds.

THE ALPHABET STORIES

The Stories of PQRST

We all have a story; we all have a story;
we all have a story.
P has a story, (tell us!). P has a story, (tell us!).
P has a story and it makes 1 sound.
P is my name (p-p). P is my name (p-p).
P is my name and I make 1 sound.

p-p-p → popcorn
p-p-p → picture
I make 1 sound.

Q has a story, (tell us!) Q has a story, (tell us!)
Q has a story and it makes 1 sound.
Q is my name (qu-qu). Q is my name (qu-qu).
Q is my name and I make 1 sound.

qu-qu-qu → quarter
qu-qu-qu → queen
I make 1 sound.

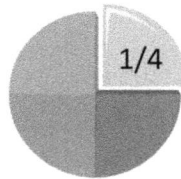

R has a story, (tell us!) R has a story, (tell us!).
R has a story and it makes 1 sound.
R is my name (r-r). R is my name (r-r).
R is my name and I make 1 sound.

r-r-r → robot
r-r-r → rake
I make 1 sound.

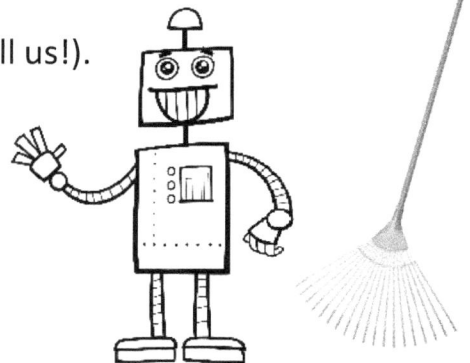

S has a story, (tell us!). S has a story, (tell us!).
S has a story and it makes 1 sound.
S is my name (s-s). S is my name (s-s).
S is my name and I make 1 sound.

s-s-s → snake
s-s-s → seal
I make 1 sound.

T has a story, (tell us!). T has a story, (tell us!).
T has a story and it makes 1 sound.
T is my name (t-t). T is my name (t-t).
T is my name and I make 1 sound.

t-t-t → tail
t-t-t → tiger
I make 1 sound.

THE ALPHABET STORIES

The Stories of FGHIJ

We all have a story; we all have a story; we all have a story.
U has a story, (tell us!). U has a story, (tell us!).
U has a story and it makes 2 sounds.
U is my name (ū-ū). U is my name (ŭ-ŭ).
U is my name and I make 2 sounds.

ū-ū-ū → unicorn
ŭ-ŭ-ŭ → up
I make 2 sounds.

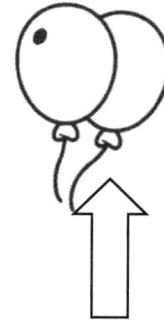

V has a story, (tell us!). V has a story, (tell us!).
V has a story and it makes 1 sound.
V is my name (v-v). V is my name (v-v).
V is my name and I make 1 sound.

v-v-v → vacuum
v-v-v → vest
I make 1 sound.

W has a story, (tell us!). W has a story (tell us!).
W has a story and it makes 1 sound.
W is my name (w-w-w). W is my name (w-w-w-w).
W is my name and I making 1 sound.

w-w-w → water
w-w-w → worm
I make 1 sound.

THE ALPHABET STORIES

X has a story, (tell us!). X has a story, (tell us!).
X has a story and it makes 2 sounds.
X is my name (x). X is my name (z-z).
X is my name and I make 2 sounds.

x-x-x → x-ray
z-z → xylophone
I make 2 sounds.

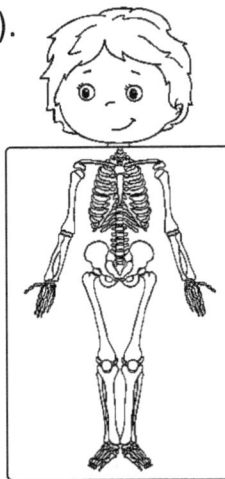

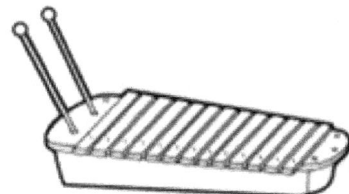

Y has a story, (tell us!). y has a story, (tell us!).
Y has a story and it makes 3 sounds.
Y is my name (y-y). Y is my name (ē-ē). Y is my name (ī-ī).
Y is my name and I make 3 sounds.

y-y-y → yoyo
ē-ē-ē → happy
ī-ī-ī → cry
I make 3 sounds.

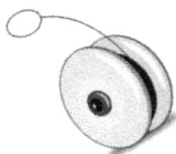

Z has a story, (tell us!). Z has a story (tell us!).
Z has a story and it makes 1 sound.
Z is my name (z-z). Z is my name (z-z-z).
Z is my name and I make 1 sound.

z-z-z → zebra
z-z-z → zipper
I make 1 sound.

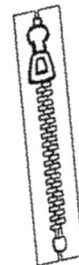

The Alphabet Stories Lyrics & Coloring Book

LETTER NAMES AND LETTER SOUNDS CHANT

Featured voice actresses/singers: M. O. Alexandre, Berlynn Eustache, Kesline Tilus

Directions: *Track* the lyrics with your finger as you sing along. *Color* the images.

Say Letter Names (Echo Letter Names)

ā/b/c/d/ē   (ā/b/c/d/ē)

f/g/h/ī/j   (f/g/h/ī/j)

k/l/m/n/ō   (k/l/m/n/ō)

p/q/r/s/t   (p/q/r/s/t)

ū/v/w/x/y/z   (ū/v/w/x/y/z)

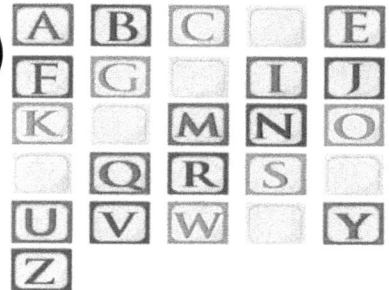

Say Letter Sounds (Echo Letter Sounds)

ă/b/c/d/ě   (ă/b/c/d/ě)

f/g/h/ĭ/j   (f/g/h/ĭ/j)

k/l/m/n/ŏ   (k/l/m/n/ŏ)

p/q/r/s/t   (p/q/r/s/t)

ŭ/v/w/x/y/z   (ŭ/v/w/x/y/z)

Say Letter Names (Echo Letter Sounds)

A B C D E

F G H I J

K L M N O

P Q R S T

U V W X Y Z

13

THE BEGINNING SOUNDS CHANT

Featured voice actresses/singers: M. O. Alexandre, Carline Antoine, Emily Aristilde, Berlynn Eustache

Directions: *Track* the lyrics with your finger as you sing along. *Color* the images.

apple 	ball 	cat 
ă/ă/ă/ă/ă	b/b/b/b/b	k/k/k/k/k/k
dog 	egg 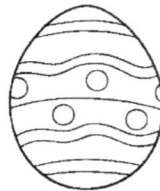	fish 
d/d/d/d/d	ĕ/ĕ/ĕ/ĕ/ĕ	f/f/f/f/f
girl 	hat 	igloo 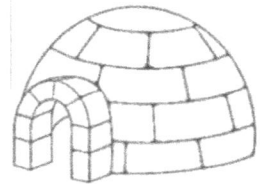
g/g/g/g/g	h/h/h/h/h	ĭ/ ĭ/ ĭ/ĭ/ĭ
jump rope 	kite 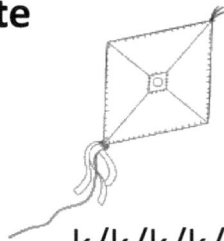	lion 
j/j/j/j/j	k/k/k/k/k	l/l/l/l/l
mouse 	nose 	octopus 
m/m/m/m/m	n/n/n/n/n	ŏ/ŏ/ŏ/ŏ/ŏ

THE BEGINNING SOUNDS CHANT

Featured voice actresses/singers: M. O. Alexandre, Carline Antoine, Emily Aristilde, Berlynn Eustache

popcorn

p/p/p/p/p

quarter

qu/qu/qu/qu/qu

rope

r/r/r/r/r

sailboat

s/s/s/s/s

tail

t/t/t/t/t

up

ŭ/ŭ/ŭ/ŭ/ŭ

vest

v/v/v/v/v

walrus

w/w/w/w/w

X-ray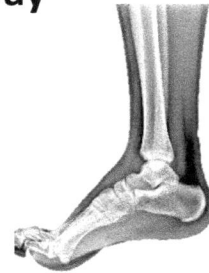

/x/

Yo-yo

y/y/y/y/y

zebra

z/z/z/z/z

THE SHORT AND LONG VOWEL CHANT

Featured voice actresses/singers: M. O. Alexandre, Carline Antoine, Berlynn Eustache

Directions: *Track* the lyrics with your finger as you sing along.

ā / ē / ī / ō / ū
ā / ē / ī / ō / ū (echo)
ā / ē / ī / ō / ū
The long vowel sounds

ă / ĕ / ĭ / ŏ / ŭ
ă / ĕ / ĭ / ŏ / ŭ (echo)
ă / ĕ / ĭ / ŏ / ŭ
The short vowel sounds

ā / ē / ī / ō / ū (3 times)
The long vowel sounds

ă / ĕ / ĭ / ŏ / ŭ (3 times)
The short vowel sounds

ā ....ē........ī........ō........ū
ă ....ĕ........ĭ........ŏ........ŭ

ā / ē / ī / ō / ū (3 times)
The long vowel sounds

ă / ĕ / ĭ / ŏ / ŭ (3 times)
The short vowel sounds

The long vowel sounds
The short vowel sounds

WHO HAS THE POWER? THE SILEN

Featured voice actresses/singers: Carline Antoine, Sophie Charles, Berlynn Eustache, Taina Salony, Tassaina Salony, Kesline Tilus

Directions: *Track* the lyrics with your finger as you sing along.

Who has the power?
Who has the power?
The silent e (2 times)
Who has the power?
Who has the power?
The silent e (2 times)

I make the **Aa** say its name.

I make the **Ee** say its name.

I make the **Ii** say its name.

I make the **Oo** say its name.

I make the **Uu** say its name.

I make them all say their names!

WHO HAS THE POWER? THE SILENT E

Featured voice actresses/singers: Carline Antoine, Sophie Charles, Berlynn Eustache, Taina Salony, Tassaina Salony, Kesline Tilus

Directions: *Track* the lyrics with your finger as you sing along.

How do you do it? (2 times)
Oh silent (e)! (2 times)
How do you do it? How do you do it?
Oh silent (e) (2 times)
I have the pattern, oh yeah (3 times)
CVCE (3 times)
Make: Let's look at the word (2 times)
Are you ready?

m
a
k
e

a consonant

a vowel

a consonant

a vowel

make

make

make

cvce

cvce

cvce

That's how I do it.
That's how I do it.
The silent (e). (2 times)

The Alphabet Stories Lyrics & Coloring Book

EE/ EA Chant (ee/ea/ai/oa/ue)

Featured voice actresses/singers: Carline Antoine, Sophie Charles, Berlynn Eustache, Taina Salony, Tassaina Salony, Kesline Tilus

Directions: *Track* the lyrics with your finger as you sing along.

Aww...

Two vowels go walking, the first one does the talking
and it usually says its name. (3 times)

ai	ai	ai
sn-ai-l	r-ai-n	br-ai-n

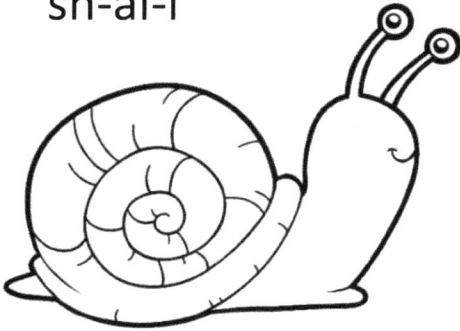  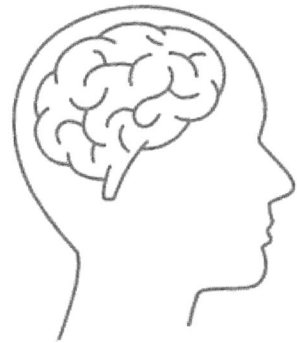

The chant!

Aww...

Two vowels go walking, the first one does the talking
And it usually says its name.

ea	ee	ea
m-ea-t	s-ee-d	r-ea-d

The chant!

EE/ EA Chant (ee/ea/ai/oa/ue)

Aww...

Two vowels go walking, the first one does the talking and it usually says its name.

oa	oa	oa
s-oa-p	r-oa-d	b-oa-t

  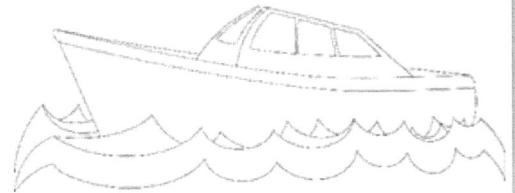

The chant! Aww...

Two vowels go walking, the first one does the talking and it usually says its name.

ue	ue	ue
cl-ue	S-ue	c-ue

The chant! Aww...

Two vowels go walking, the first one does the talking and it usually says its name. (2 times)

Aww... The chant!

NAUGHTY PAULINA (au/aw

Featured voice actresses/singers: Daphney Charles, Sophie Charles, Berlynn Eustache,
Gina Rodriguez, Taina Salony, Tassaina Salony, Kesline Tilus

Directions: *Track* the lyrics with your finger as you sing along.

Get your paws out of the sauce.
Get your claws out of the sauce.
Oh, how awful Paulina!
(2 times)

Refrain
Naughty Paulina! (2 times)
You've been taught.
You're at fault. Paulina!
(2 times)

It's a fact we all have flaws!
It's a fact we all have faults.
Oh, how dreadful Paulina!
(2 times)

Whenever you take a pause
Knowing you shall be lauded,
Oh, how truthful Paulina!
(2 times)

Be nice! Be nice! Be nice!
Paulina. (2 times)

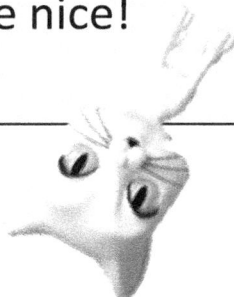

LLOYD THE ROYAL BUTLER?

Featured voice actresses/actors: Gerardson Alexandre, Sophie Charles, Richard Saber, Taina Salony, Tassaina Salony

Directions: *Track* the dialogues with your finger as you play along.

1 Whose Lloyd you say?

2 Lloyd is the Tin Toy Boy. Appoint him as the royal butler. Appoint him as the royal butler, I say.

3 Lloyd the Tin Toy Boy?

4 I know he's like an android. But think about it; we can't avoid the choice. Appoint him as the royal butler. Lloyd is humanoid. Lloyd is dexterous. Lloyd is adroit.

5 His boyish good looks, will serve him well. Appoint him as the royal butler.

6 Sure he has some foibles. Sure he might be spoiled.

7 Deploy Lloyd, I say, as the royal butler.

8 Lloyd the Tin Toy Boy, you are thereby dubbed the Royal Butler!

Yeah!!!

9 Raise your voice! Make some noise! Don't be poised! Rejoice for Lloyd as the royal butler!

(Applause)

BUTLER LLOYD (oi/oy)

Featured Singer: Daphney Charles

Directions: Track the lyrics with your finger as you sing along.

coil

boil

Butler Lloyd
Butler Lloyd, Butler Lloyd,
could you oil the coil for me?
Butler Lloyd, what a joy,
when you oil the coil for me.

Refrain
Oil, oil, oil the coil oil the coil for me
Oil, oil, oil the coil oil the coil for me

Butler Lloyd can't you hear
how the coil is so noisy.
And the noise won't annoy
when the coil is oiled, you'll see.

Butler Lloyd will rejoice
and the joy will set you free.
And the king will employ
and reward your loyalty.

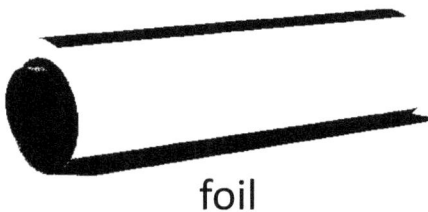

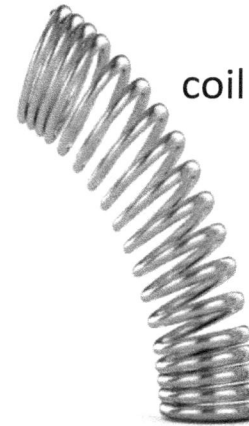

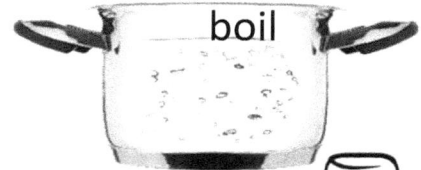

Oil

Lloyd

foil

23

THE OUCH CHANT (ou/ow)

Featured voice actress/singer: M. O. Alexandre, Carline Antoine

Ouch! Ouch!
The porcupine's stinging,
Ouch! Ouch!
The cactuses pricking,
Ouch! Ouch!
The sword is piercing,
Bring forth a pain to my heart.

Shout! Shout!
The cloud has receded.
Shout! Shout!
The bud has sprouted.
Shout! Shout!
The sound resounded,
Bring forth a song to my heart.

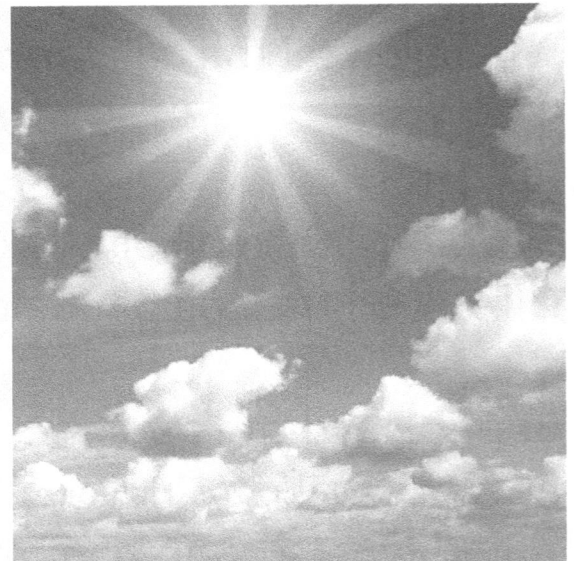

Wow! Wow!
My birthday is coming,
Wow! Wow!
The presents arriving,
Wow! Wow!
The party's amazing,
Bring forth a cheer to my heart.
Bring forth a cheer to my heart.
Bring forth a cheer to my heart.
Bring forth a cheer to my heart.
SHOUT!

AMAZING!

THE R-CONROLLED VOWEL SKIT

Featured voice actresses/ actors /singers: Gerardson Alexandre, Carline Antoine, Emily Aristilde, Gregory Aristilde, Sophie Charles, Taina Salony, Tassaina Salony

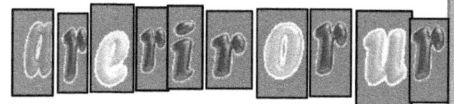

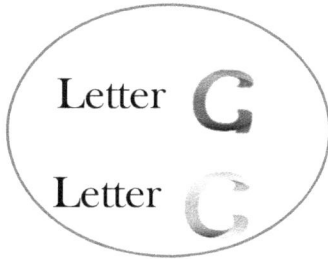

areriroruur

Letter **G**
Letter **C**

Vowels
u a
o i e

1 Good morning vowels!
(3 times)

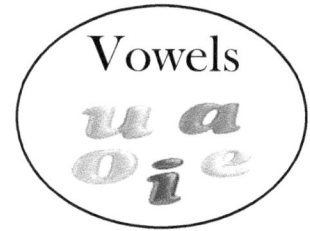

3 What is the matter?
You don't sound happy today?
What is the matter?

2 Good morning
Letter G.
Good morning
Letter C.

We are being controlled by the letter R. 4

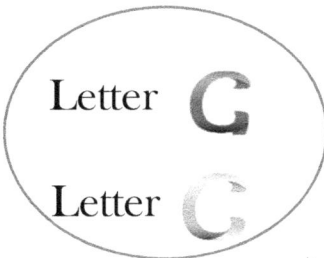

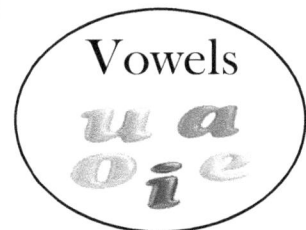

Vowels
u a
o i e

Letter **G**
Letter **C**

5 What?
R is controlling you too?

6 Yes, R is controlling us. You know that we usually make the short vowel sound (ă / ĕ/ ĭ / ŏ / ŭ). But when R comes along, it makes us say:

25

THE R-CONROLLED VOWEL SKIT

Vowels
u a o i e

7 ar er ir or ur

Letter
a

8 I want to say ă instead I say:

ar

Letter
e

9 I want to say ě instead I say:

er

Letter
i

10 I want to say ĭ instead I say:

ir

Letter
o

11 I want to say ŏ instead I say:

or

Letter
u

12 I want to say ŭ instead I say:

ur

Letter C
Letter C

13 Aaah, I see.

THE R-CONROLLED VOWEL SKIT

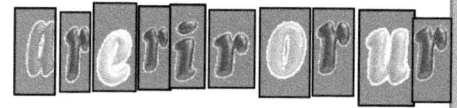

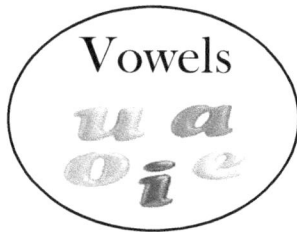

Vowels
u a
o i e

14 — R
is controlling us!
That's why we're
so sad.

Letter **G**

15 — I can understand letter A and letter U
being sad because they are being controlled
by the letter R,
but you, letter E, I,
and your cousin Y,
you do the same thing to us.
You have no right to be sad?

Letter **C**

16 — Yea, you're right. When E, I, or Y comes along,
letter G cannot make the hard g sound (g/g/g)
that it usually makes,
and I cannot make the hard c sound (k/k/k)
that I usually make.
Letter G has to make the soft g sound (j/j/j)
and I have to make the soft c sound (s/s/s).

Vowels
u a o i e

ar er ir or ur

Letter C

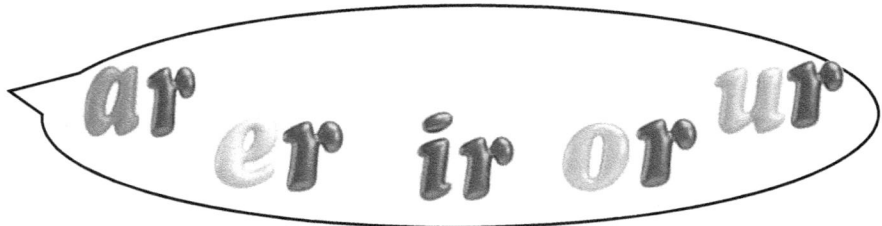

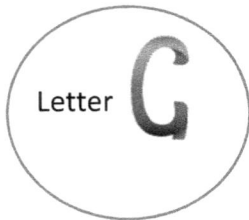

17 Letter C, remind me again of that little chant that helped us remember how we're being controlled by: e, i, or y

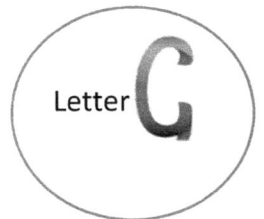

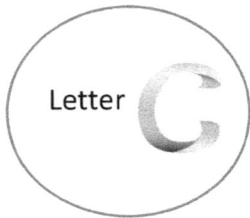

Letter C

Letter C

18
What little chant?

19
You know, The Soft C and the Soft G chant.

20
Oh, Ok! Let's go!

u a o i e

THE SOFT C CHANT

Featured voice actresses/singers: M. O. Alexandre, Carline Antoine, Emily Aristilde, Sophie Charles, Taina Salony, Tassaina Salony

Directions: *Track* the lyrics with your finger as you sing along.

Sometimes the C says s/s/s, s/s/s, s/s/s.
Sometimes the C says s/s/s.
I'll tell you why!

If after the C
there's an /e/ or an /i/ or a /y/ (3 times)

They all make the C say s/s/s/.
I'll show you how.

cent

circus

cymbal

They all make the C say s/s/s/.
You give it a try!

THE SOFT C CHANT

Featured voice actresses/singers: M. O. Alexandre, Carline Antoine, Emily Aristilde, Sophie Charles, Taina Salony, Tassaina Salony

Instrumental Music   **(Sing along to the tune of the music)**

cent

circus

cymbal

Sometimes the C says s/s/s, s/s/s, s/s/s.
Sometimes the C says s/s/s.

Now you know why!

ce
ci
cy

THE SOFT G CHANT

Featured voice actresses/singers: M. O. Alexandre, Carline Antoine, Emily Aristilde, Sophie Charles, Taina Salony, Tassaina Salony

Directions: *Track* the lyrics with your finger as you sing along.

Sometimes the G says j/j/j, j/j/j, j/j/j.
Sometimes the G says j/j/j.
I'll tell you why!

If after the G
there's an /e/ or an /i/ or a /y/ (3 times)

They all make the G say j/j/j.
I'll show you how.

ge
gi
gy

gem

giant

gym

You give it a try!

Instrumental Music

THE SOFT G CHANT

Featured voice actresses/singers: M. O. Alexandre, Carline Antoine, Emily Aristilde, Sophie Charles, Taina Salony, Tassaina Salony

Instrumental Music **(Sing along to the tune of the music)**

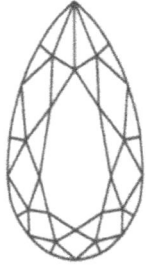

gem

giant

gym

Sometimes the G says j/j/j, j/j/j, j/j/j.
Sometimes the G says j/j/j.

Now you know why!

ge
gi
gy

PHONOMOJO & THE PHONICS OUTLAW

Featured voice actresses/actors: Gerardson Alexandre, Emily Aristilde, Jackson Lubke, Frank Pagliaro, Lilia Turenne, Richard Saber

Directions: *Track* the dialogues with your finger as you play along.

PhonoMojo here, at the service of the Phonics King

2

1 PhonoMojo, I am Lloyd the Royal Butler. The King has asked me to summon you here for a special mission.

3 PhonoMojo! this is the greatest mission I've ever given you. I want you to go to the hills, the valleys, and the mountains. Go to the plateaus, the plains, and the canyons. Go to the desserts, the lakes, and the rivers. Go all over the world; gather me all the phonics outlaws.
Butler Lloyd, tell him, who are the phonics outlaws.

PHONOMOJO & THE PHONICS OUTLAW

Featured voice actresses/actors: Gerardson Alexandre, Emily Aristilde, Jackson Lubke, Frank Pagliaro, Lilia Turenne, Richard Saber

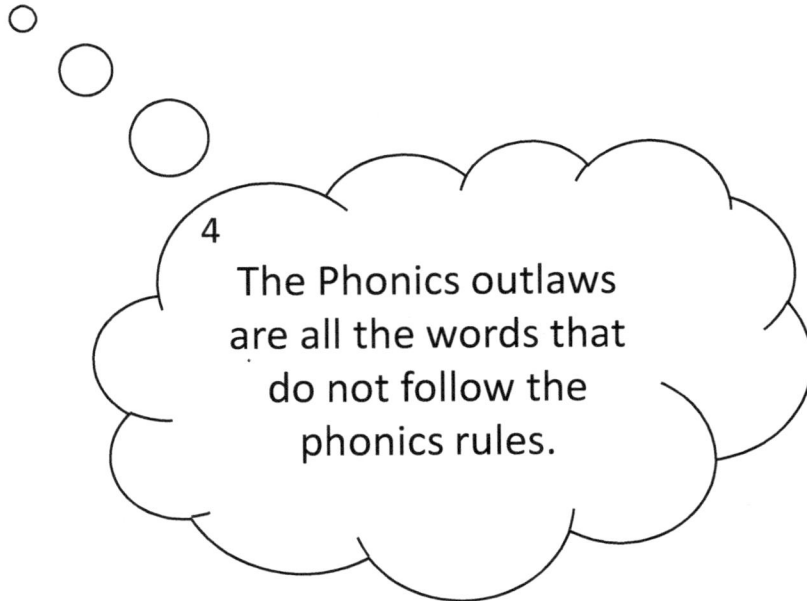

4

The Phonics outlaws are all the words that do not follow the phonics rules.

5

Exactly, I want you to bring them here to join me along with the words that do follow the phonics rules. Bring them all here for the greatest phonics celebration that the world has ever seen.
Now, Go!

6

Drum roll!

PHONOMOJO & THE PHONICS OUTLAW

Featured voice actresses/actors: Gerardson Alexandre, Emily Aristilde, Jackson Lubke, Frank Pagliaro, Lilia Turenne, Richard Saber

1 This is PhonoMojo, making a roll call to the phonics outlaws.

2 Bread

3 Sir, yes Sir!

Present and accounted for, Sir

4 Pear

5

6 Moose

8 spoon

7 Sir, yes Sir!

Present and accounted for, Sir

9

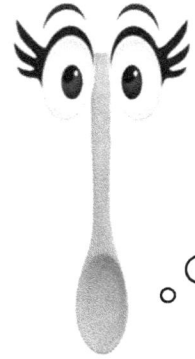

10 This is your leader, PhonoMojo speaking, now let's march!

Left, Left, left, right left (3 times)

PHONOMOJO & THE PHONICS OUTLAW

Featured voice actresses/actors: Gerardson Alexandre, Emily Aristilde, Jackson Lubke, Frank Pagliaro, Lilia Turenne, Richard Saber

1 This is PhonoMojo. Are those fellow phonics outlaws I see?

4 Coil?

2 Coin, is that you?

5 Present and accounted for, Sir.

3 Sir, yes Sir!

6 Mouse?

8 Cloud?

7 Sir, yes Sir!

9 Present and accounted for, Sir!

10 We got a fine group of phonics outlaws here. Let's go rally up some more! Now let's march!

11 PhonoMojo is surely rallying up a lot of phonics outlaws. Why don't you round-up some of your own?

Left, Left, left, right left (3 times)

The Alphabet Stories Lyrics & Coloring Book

CONSONANT DIAGRAPHS!

Featured voice actresses /singers: M.O. Alexandre, Emily Aristilde, Carline Antoine, Sophie Charles, Berlynn Eustache, Taina Salony, Tassaina Salony

Directions: *Track* the lyrics with your finger as you sing along.

What is it?

A digraph, it's a consonant digraph. (2 times)

/th/ /th/ /th/   TH   (2 times)
/th/ /th/ /th/ /th/   TH

this	that	those

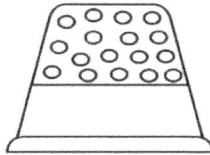

/th/ /th/ /th /, /th/ /th/ /th/ /th/ (2 times)

What is it?

A digraph, it's a consonant digraph. (2 times)

/ch/ /ch/ /ch/   CH   (2 times)
/ch/ /ch/ /ch/ /ch/   CH

cheese	chip	chop

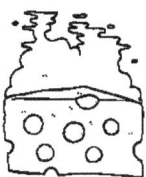

/ch/ /ch/ /ch/, /ch/ /ch/ /ch/ /ch/ (2 times)

37

CONSONANT DIAGRAPHS!

Featured voice actresses /singers: M.O. Alexandre, Emily Aristilde, Carline Antoine, Sophie Charles, Berlynn Eustache, Taina Salony, Tassaina Salony

What is it?

A digraph, it's a consonant digraph. (2 times)

/wh/ /wh/ /wh/	WH (2 times)
/wh/ /wh/ /wh/ /wh/	WH

what	where	when

wh/ /wh/ /wh /, /wh/ /wh/ /wh/ /wh/ (2 times)

What is it?

A digraph, it's a consonant digraph. (2 times)

/sh/ /sh/ /sh/ /sh/ /sh/ /sh/ /sh/
/sh/ /sh/ /sh/

shed	ship	shop

/sh/ /sh/ /sh/, /sh/ /sh/ /sh/ /sh/ (2 times)

The Alphabet Stories Lyrics & Coloring Book

CONSONANT DIAGRAPHS!

Featured voice actresses /singers: M.O. Alexandre, Emily Aristilde, Carline Antoine,
Sophie Charles, Berlynn Eustache, Taina Salony, Tassaina Salony

/th/ /th/ /th/ /th/ /th/ /th/ /th/
/th/ /th/ /th/
/th/ /th/ /th/ /th/

/ch/ /ch/ /ch/, /ch/ /ch/ /ch/ /ch/
/ch/ /ch/ /ch/
/ch/ /ch/ /ch/ /ch/

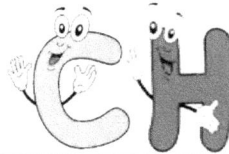

/wh/ /wh/ /wh/, /wh/ /wh/ /wh/ /wh/
/wh/ /wh/ /wh/
/wh/ /wh/ /wh/ /wh/

/sh/ /sh/ /sh/, /sh/ /sh/ /sh/ /sh/
/sh/ /sh/ /sh/
/sh/ /sh/ /sh/ /sh/

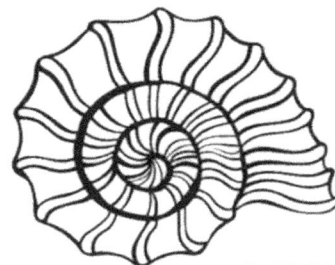

What are they ?

They're digraphs.
They're consonant digraphs!   (2 times)

THE GONG SONG (-ng)

Featured singers: M.O. Alexandre, Sophie Charles, Guerlens Desir,
Berlynn Eustache, Taina Salony, Tassaina Salony

Directions: Track the lyrics with your finger as you sing along.

Refrain

YOU can never go wrong with a Gong Song.
YOU can never ever go wrong with a Gong Song.
YOU can never ever go wrong with a Gong Song.
Know you'll always belong.

Whenever you're singing a song.
It may seem ever so long.
Even when it's an hour long.
Know you'll never be wrong.

What a wondrous wonderful thing.
Whenever, you're starting to sing.
No matter where you're singing.
A gong song is amusing.

YOU can never go wrong with a Gong Song.
YOU can never go wrong with a Gong Song.
YOU can never go wrong with a Gong Song.
You can never go wrong with a Gong SONG.

THE BUBBLE GAME (-le)

Featured voice actresses/ actors: Gerardson Alexandre, Xavier Brown, Lilia Turenne, Nelson Val

Directions: *Track* the words with your finger as you play along.

1 The Bubble Game?

2 We love the Bubble game!

3 Let's play the bubble game! Too-doo (2 times)

4 Will we get a chance to play?

5
bubble .. apple

feeble .. people

jungle .. beetle

double .. trouble

middle .. riddle

6
cobble .. ruffle

tickle .. cattle

cradle .. battle

angle .. nimble

little .. able

7 Let's play the bubble game! Too-doo (2 times)

41

THE BUBBLE GAME (-le)

Featured voice actresses/ actors: Gerardson Alexandre, Xavier Brown, Lilia Turenne, Nelson Val

Let's play the bubble game! Too-doo (2 times) 8

Okay, those were some good words. Now, it's your turn. Ready. Set. Go! 9

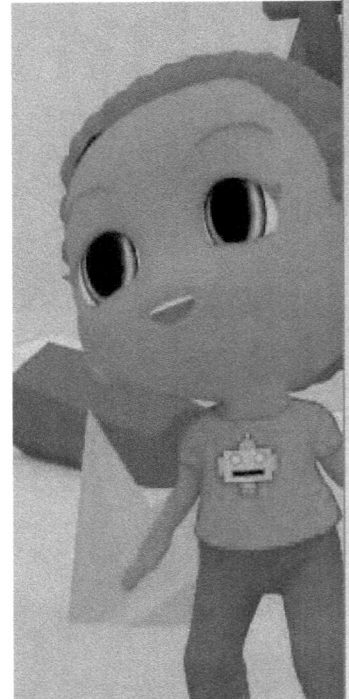

terrible .. rumble

horrible .. rubble 10

poodle .. puddle

dabble .. feeble

muffle .. snuffle

dribble .. scribble

11 scrabble .. noodle

sparkle .. beagle

bundle .. circle

ankle .. single

THE BUBBLE GAME (-le)

Featured voice actresses/ actors: Gerardson Alexandre, Xavier Brown, Lilia Turenne, Nelson Val

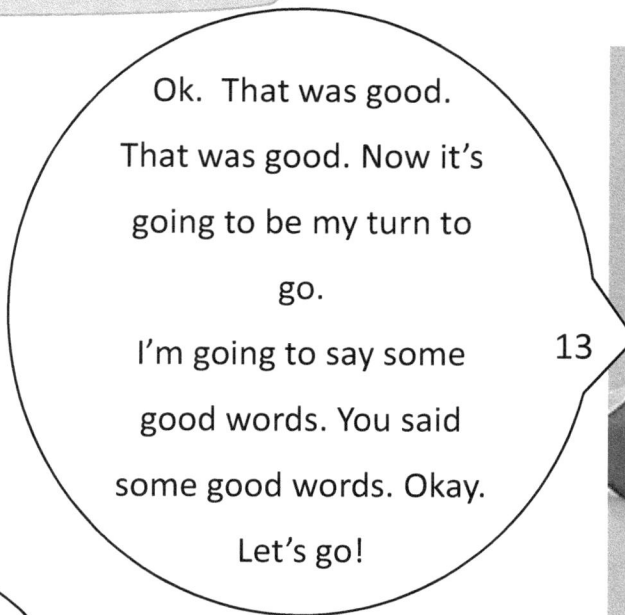

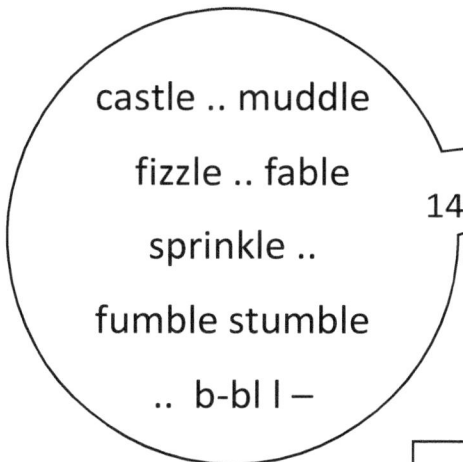

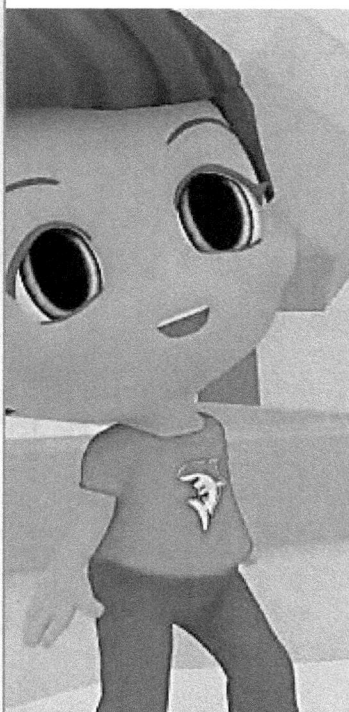

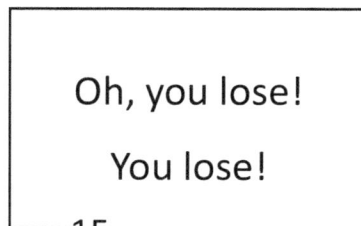

12 Let's play the bubble game! Too-doo (2 times)

13 Ok. That was good. That was good. Now it's going to be my turn to go.
I'm going to say some good words. You said some good words. Okay. Let's go!

14 castle .. muddle
fizzle .. fable
sprinkle ..
fumble stumble
.. b-bl l —

15 Oh, you lose! You lose!

16 Ok! Let's play it again!

17 It's our turn!

18 Let's play the bubble game! Too-doo.

Phonics Celebration Extra Practice Exercises

Say the name of each picture. Color the pictures that begin with the letter Aa. Trace the letter Aa.

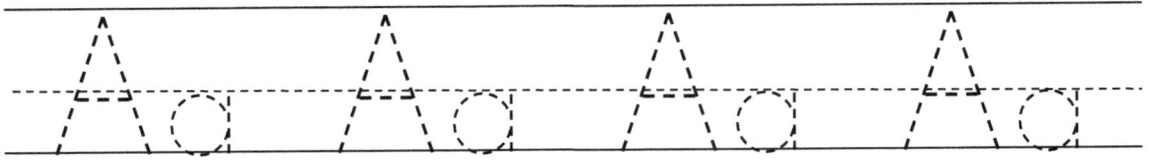

A A A A A A

Aa Aa Aa Aa

ant

apple

arrow

Aa

anchor

ball

alligator

Phonics Celebration Extra Practice Exercises

Say the name of each picture. Color the pictures that begin with the letter Bb. Trace the letter Bb.

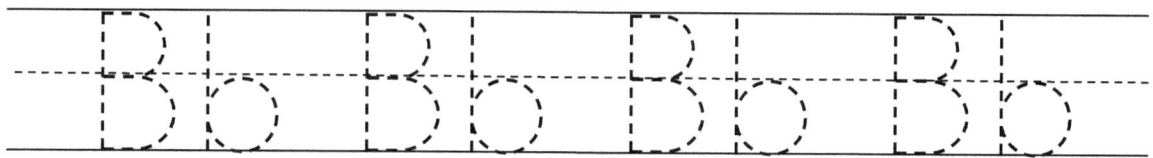

bat

bee

bike

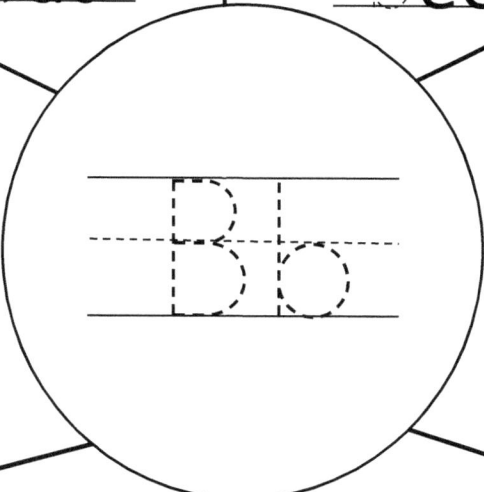

Bb

award

boat

butterfly

Phonics Celebration Extra Practice Exercises

Say the name of each picture. Color the pictures that begin with the letter Cc. Trace the letter Cc.

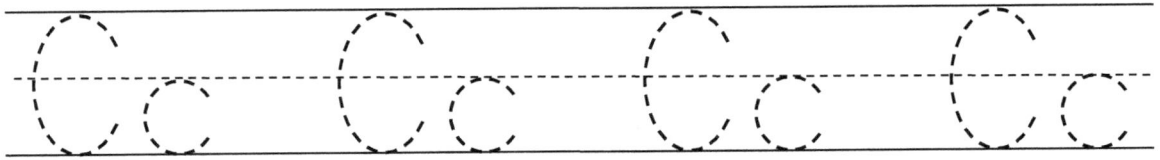

crayons

cow

cat

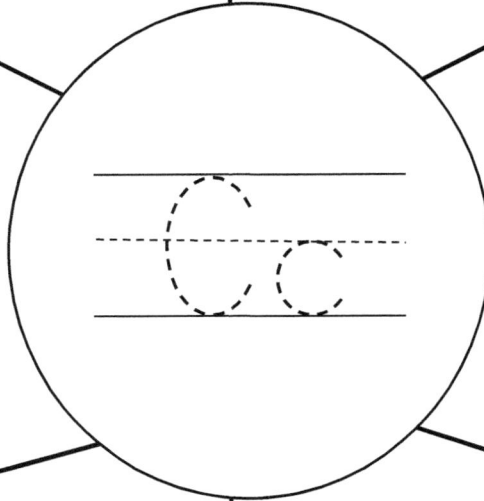

Cc

dog

camel

kangaroo

Phonics Celebration Extra Practice Exercises

Say the name of each picture. Color the pictures that begin with the letter Dd. Trace the letter Dd.

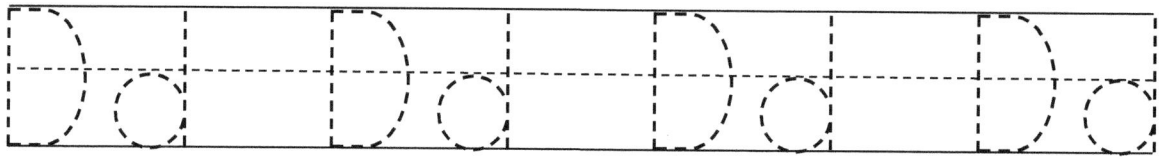

Dd Dd Dd Dd

dinosaur   deer

Dd

bat   duck

dragonfly   dolphin

Phonics Celebration Extra Practice Exercises

Say the name of each picture. Color the pictures that begin with the letter Ee. Trace the letter Ee.

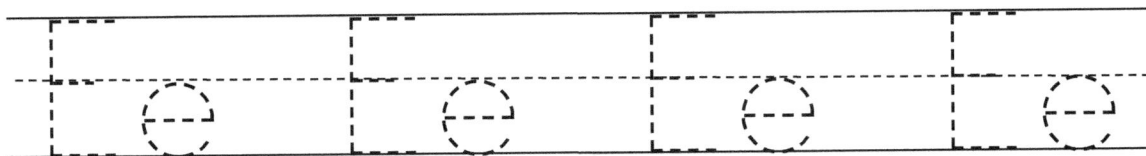

escalator

fan

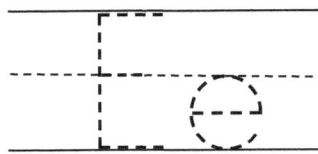

elbow

elk

elevator

elephant

Phonics Celebration Extra Practice Exercises

Say the name of each picture. Color the pictures that begin with the letter Ff. Trace the letter Ff.

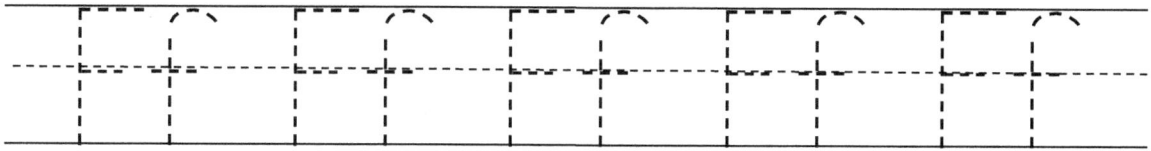

frog

egg

flower

Ff

ox

fish

fork

Phonics Celebration Extra Practice Exercises

Say the name of each picture. Color the pictures that begin with the letter Gg. Trace the letter Gg.

Gg Gg Gg Gg

 goat

 gem

 guitar

 gift

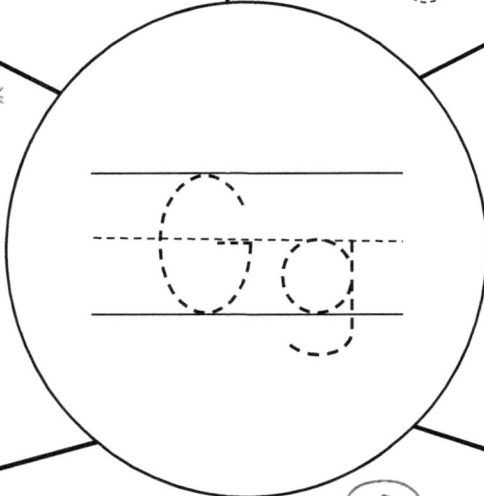 Gg

 hat

 goose

Phonics Celebration Extra Practice Exercises

Say the name of each picture. Color the pictures that begin with the letter Hh. Trace the letter Hh.

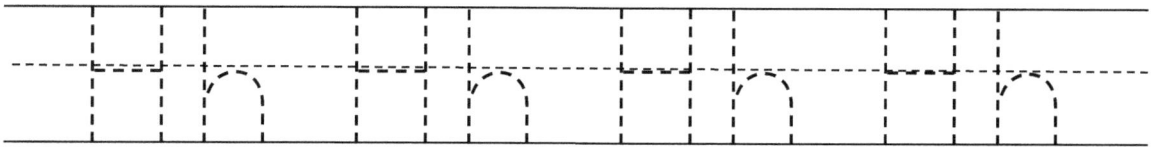

gloves

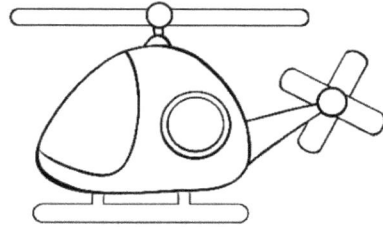

helicopter

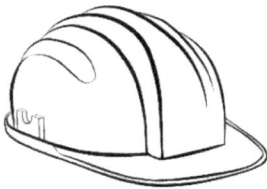

helmet

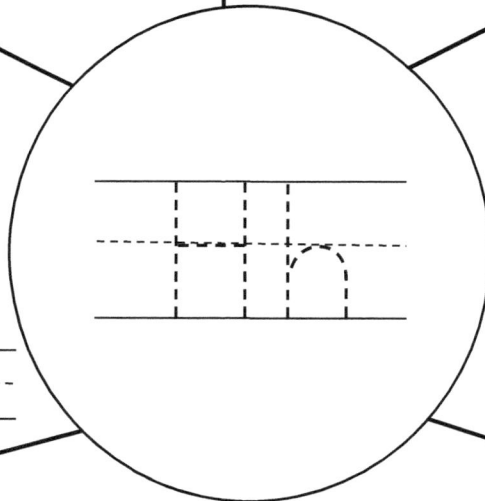

house

hammer

horse

Phonics Celebration Extra Practice Exercises

Say the name of each picture. Color the pictures that begin with the letter Ii. Trace the letter Ii.

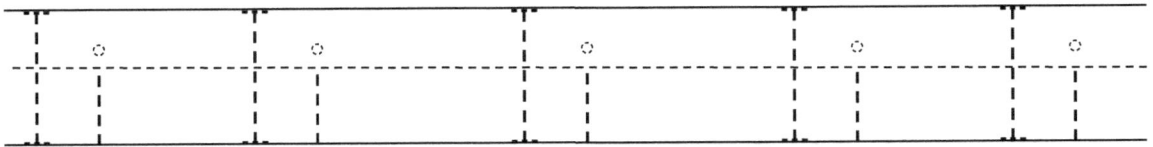

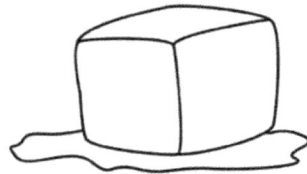

ice

jar

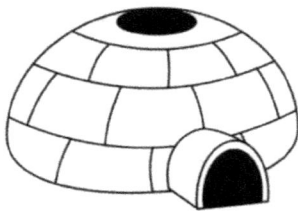

gloo

vy

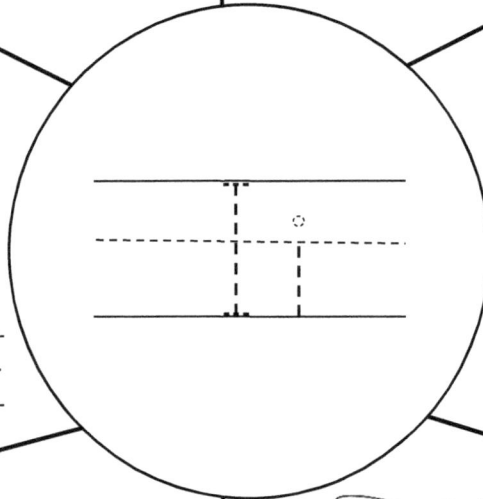

guana

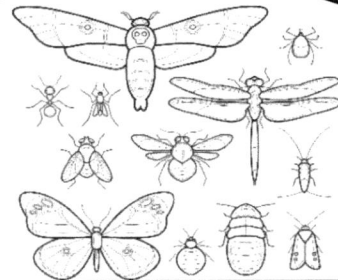

nsects

Phonics Celebration Extra Practice Exercises

Say the name of each picture. Color the pictures that begin with the letter Jj. Trace the letter Jj.

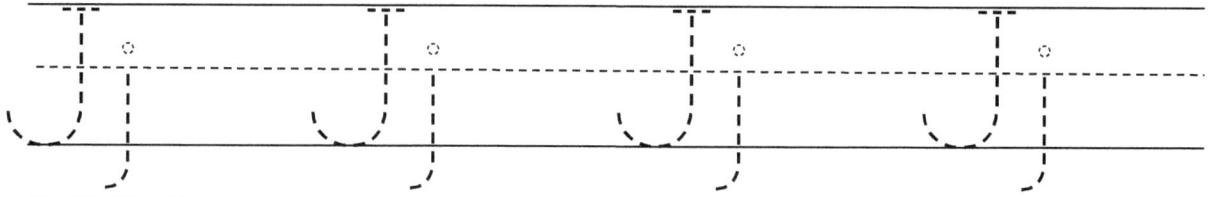

jet

jacket

jellyfish

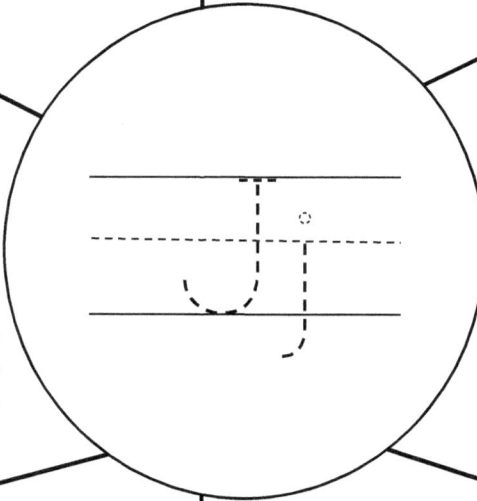

Jj

jeep

ice cream

jump rope

Phonics Celebration Extra Practice Exercises

Say the name of each picture. Color the pictures that begin with the letter Kk. Trace the letter Kk.

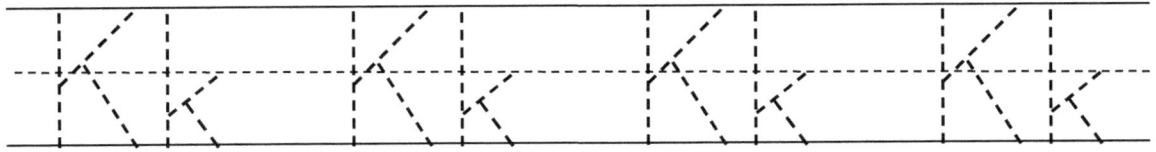

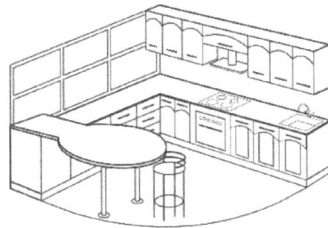

itchen

angaroo

ey

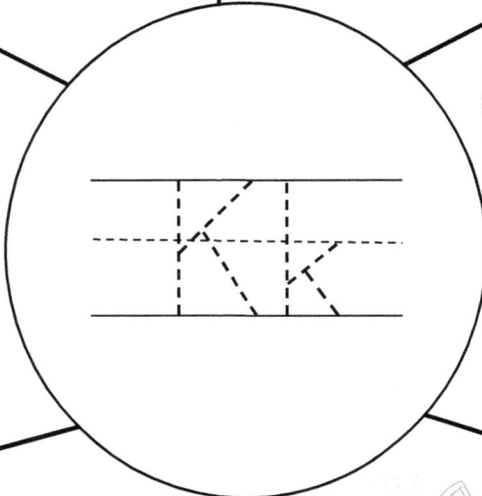

ion

ettle

itten

Phonics Celebration Extra Practice Exercises

Say the name of each picture. Color the pictures that begin with the letter Ll. Trace the letter Ll.

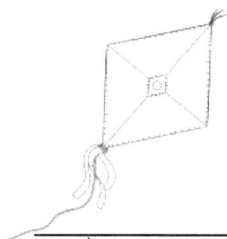

kite

ladybug

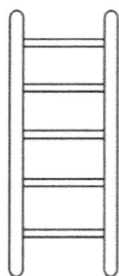

adder

eaf

amb

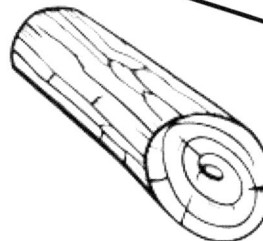

og

Phonics Celebration Extra Practice Exercises

Say the name of each picture. Color the pictures that begin with the letter Mm. Trace the letter Mm.

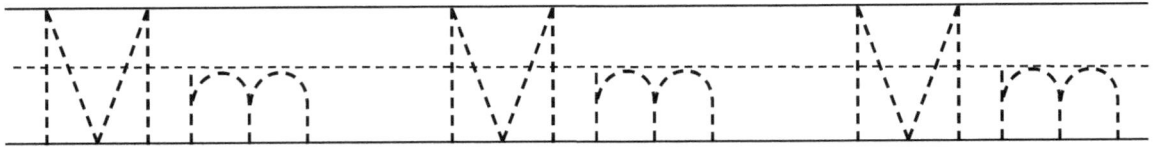

Mm Mm Mm

nose

ushroom

oth

Mm

onkey

eat

oon

Phonics Celebration Extra Practice Exercises

Say the name of each picture. Color the pictures that begin with the letter Nn. Trace the letter Nn.

Nn Nn Nn Nn

nest

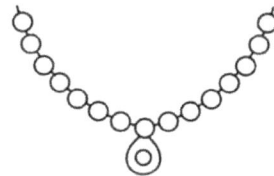

necklace

nurse

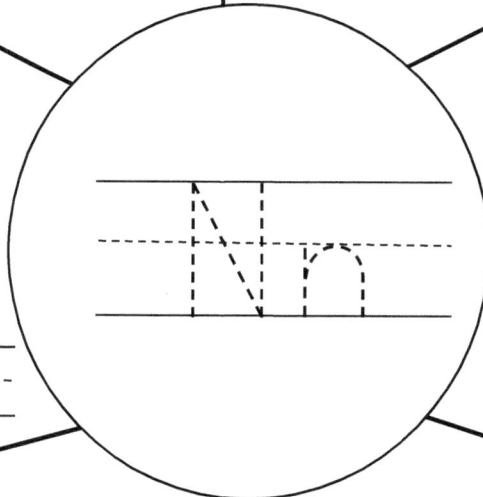

Nn

mouse

9

nine

numbers

Phonics Celebration Extra Practice Exercises

Say the name of each picture. Color the pictures that begin with the letter Oo. Trace the letter Oo.

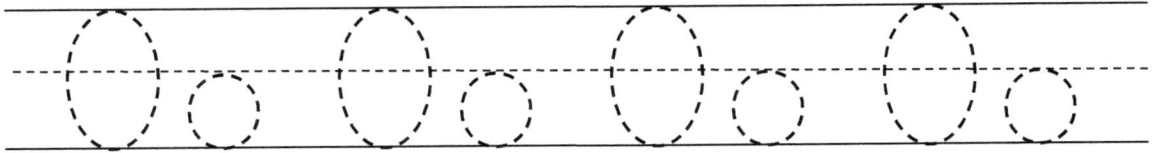

pig

octopus

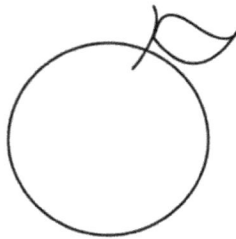

orange

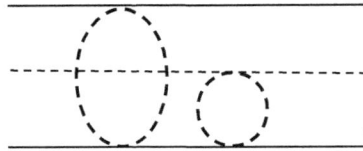

Oo

olives

ostrich

orchid

Phonics Celebration Extra Practice Exercises

Say the name of each picture. Color the pictures that begin with the letter Pp. Trace the letter Pp.

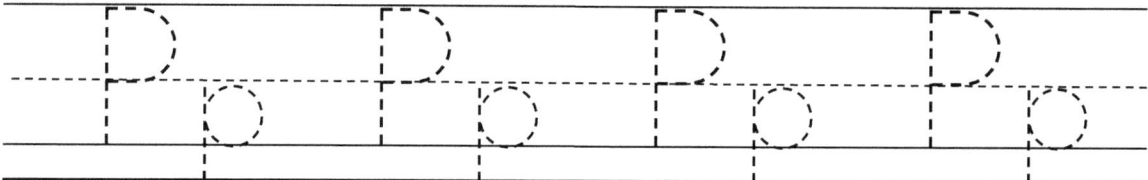

 penguin

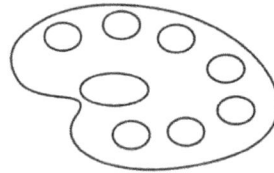 palette

 panda

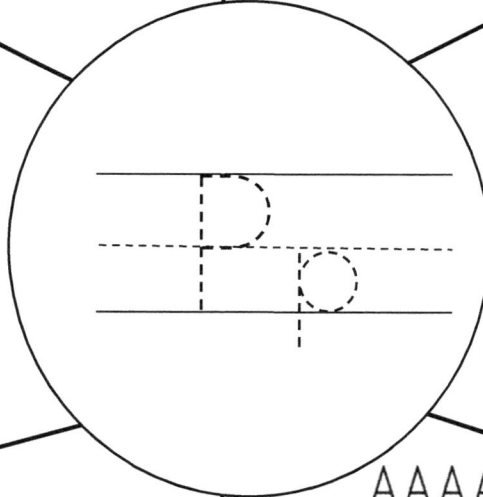

 owl

 pie

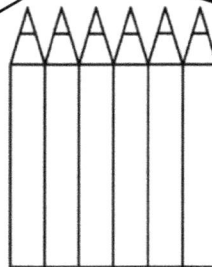 pencils

Phonics Celebration Extra Practice Exercises

Say the name of each picture. Color the pictures that begin with the letter Qq. Trace the letter Qq.

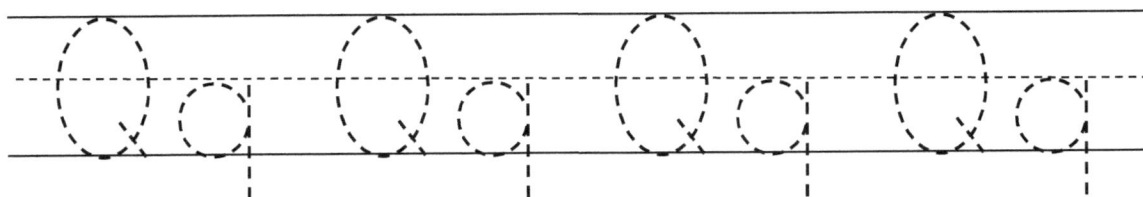

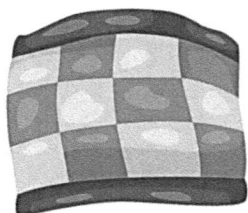

quilt

quarter

quail

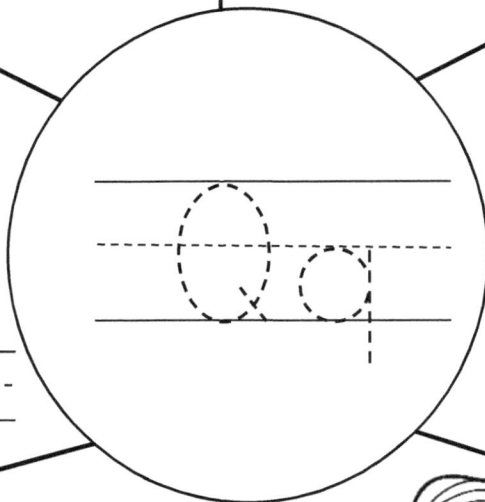

queen

quartz

rose

Phonics Celebration Extra Practice Exercises

Say the name of each picture. Color the pictures that begin with the letter Rr. Trace the letter Rr.

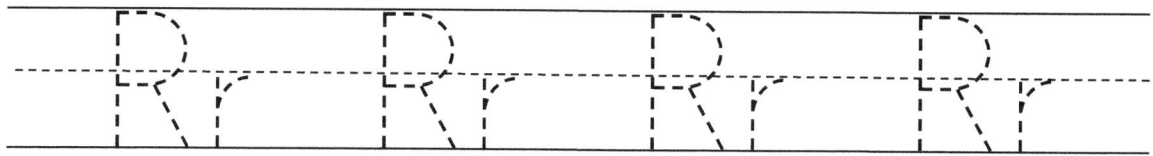

attle

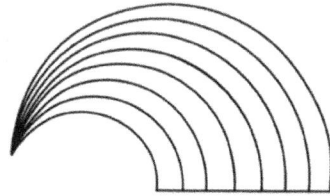
ainbow

abbit

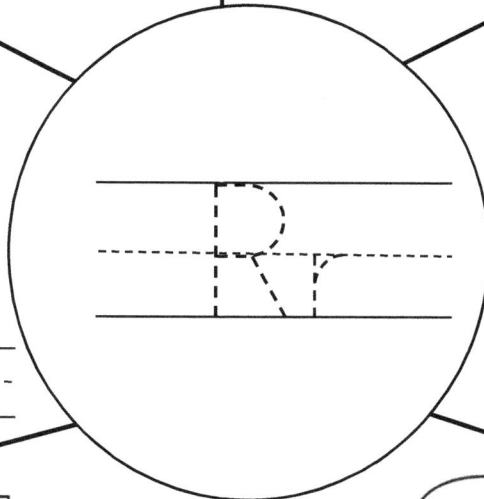

at

obot

question mark

Phonics Celebration Extra Practice Exercises

Say the name of each picture. Color the pictures that begin with the letter Ss. Trace the letter Ss.

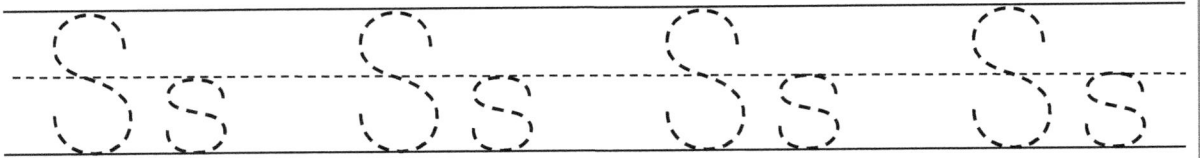

Ss Ss Ss Ss

sheep

stars

sailboat

Ss

tree

seal

swan

Phonics Celebration Extra Practice Exercises

Say the name of each picture. Color the pictures that begin with the letter Tt. Trace the letter Tt.

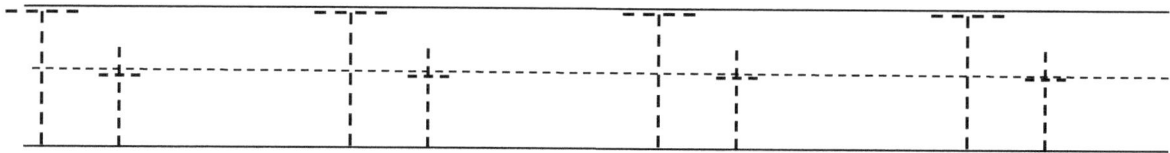

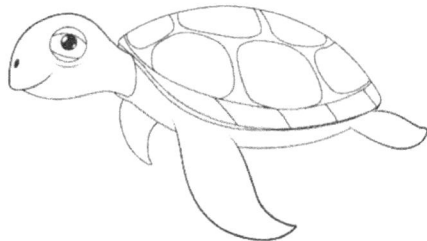

urtle

ractor

omato

sun

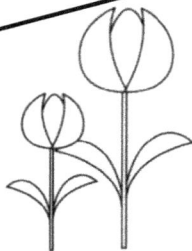

ulips

iger

Phonics Celebration Extra Practice Exercises

Say the name of each picture. Color the pictures that begin with the letter Uu. Trace the letter Uu.

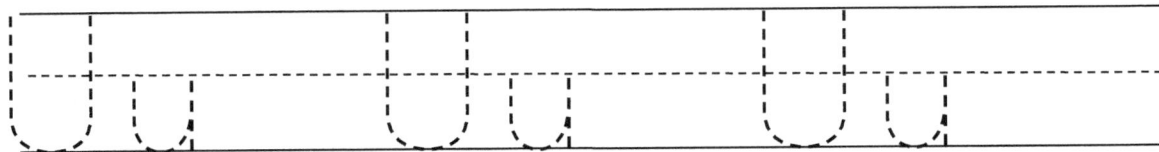

unicorn

unlock

tomato

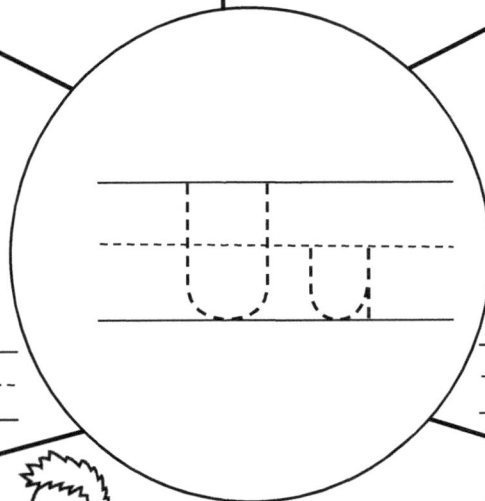

utencils

unicycle

unhappy

Phonics Celebration Extra Practice Exercises

Say the name of each picture. Color the pictures that begin with the letter Vv. Trace the letter Vv.

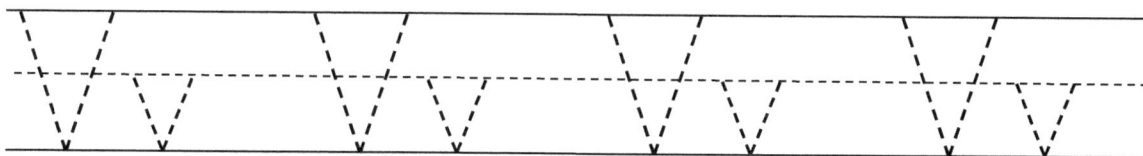

ᐯᐯᐯᐯᐯᐯᐯᐯᐯ

violin   umbrella

van   vase

vowels   vulture

Phonics Celebration Extra Practice Exercises

Say the name of each picture. Color the pictures that begin with the letter Ww. Trace the letter Ww.

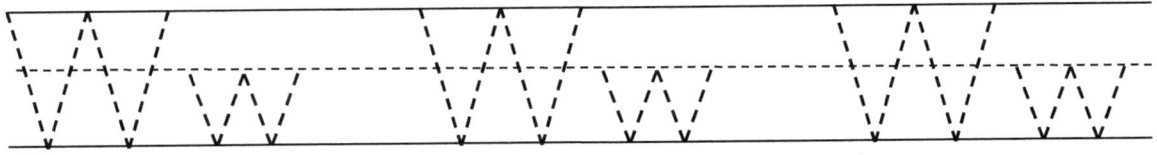

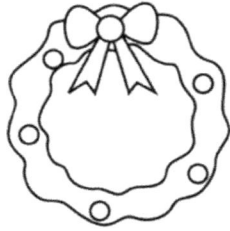

wreath

wolf

window

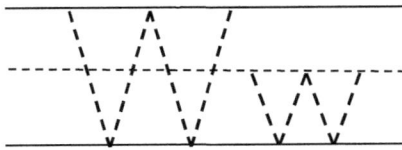

wand

watermelon

vegetables

Phonics Celebration Extra Practice Exercises

Say the name of each picture. Color the pictures that begin with the letter Xx. Trace the letter Xx.

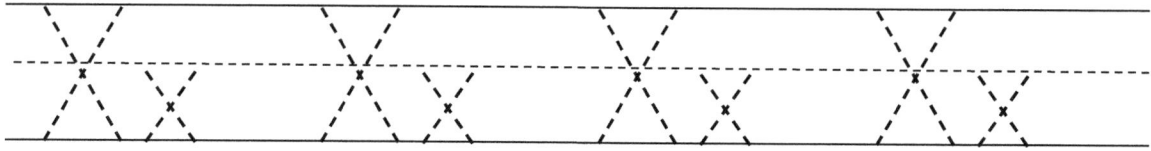

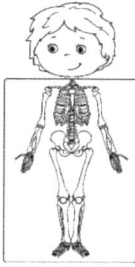

x-ray

x-ray fish

fox

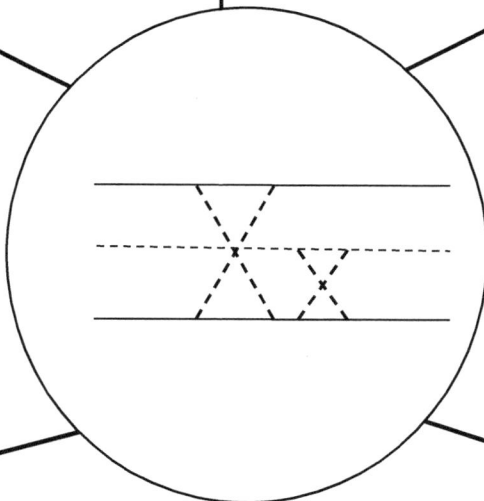

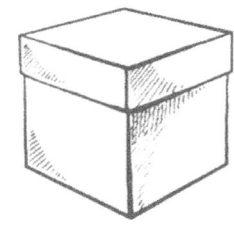

box

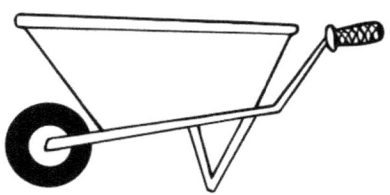

wheelbarrow

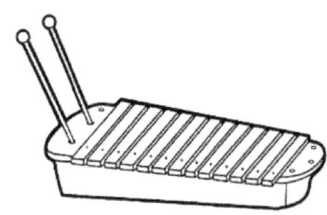

xylophone

Phonics Celebration Extra Practice Exercises

Say the name of each picture. Color the pictures that begin with the letter Yy. Trace the letter Yy.

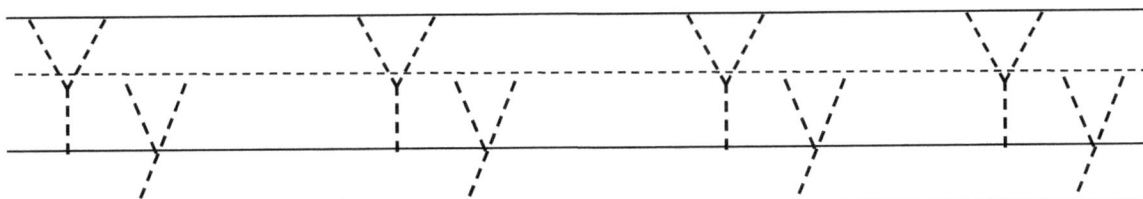

 yatch

 yarn

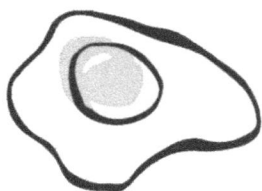 yolk

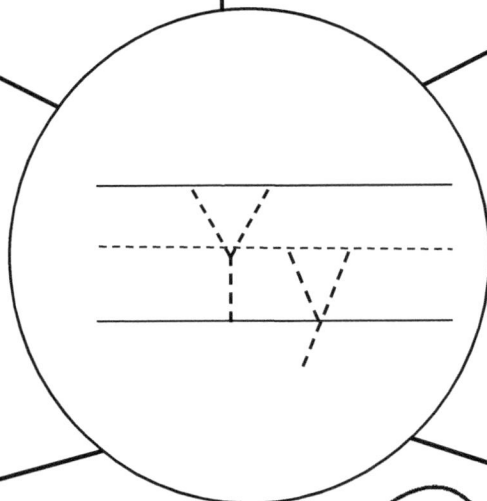 Yy

six

 yogurt

 yak

Phonics Celebration Extra Practice Exercises

Say the name of each picture. Color the pictures that begin with the letter Zz. Trace the letter Zz.

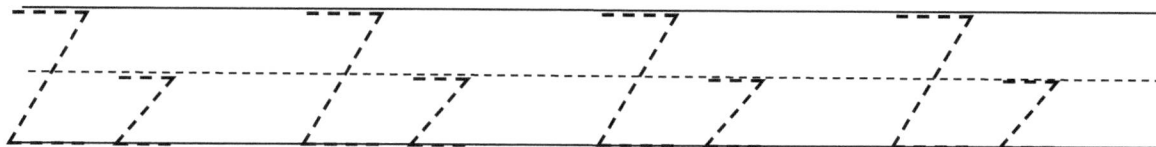

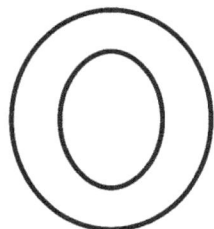

_ero

_ebra

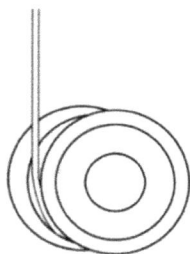

_oyo

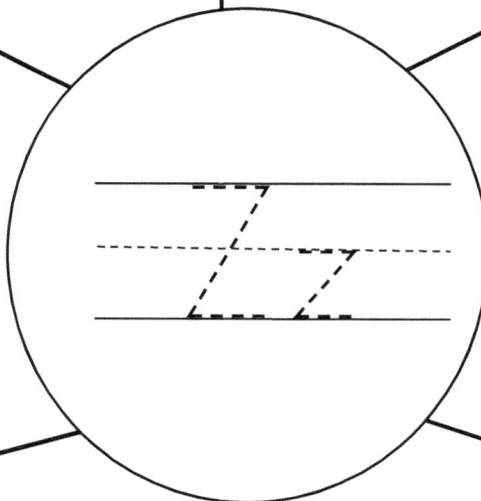

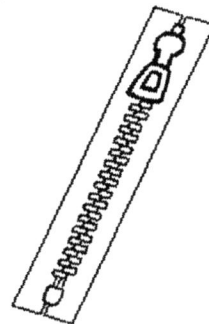

_ipper

_oo

_ucchini

The Silent (e) Extra Practice
Read the words.
Color the pictures.

e

Patterns

CVC	CVCE
a cap	cape
e pet	Pete
i kit	kite
o Rob	robe
u cub	cube

The R-Controlled Vowels Extra Practice: Trace the letters. Read the words. Color the pictures.

ar	→	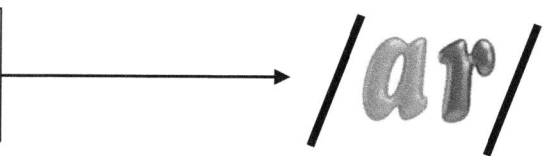

c a r

er	→	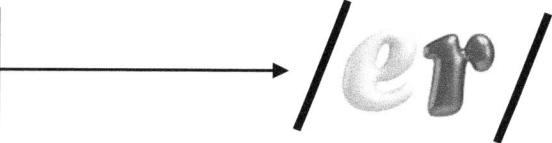

feath e r

ir	→	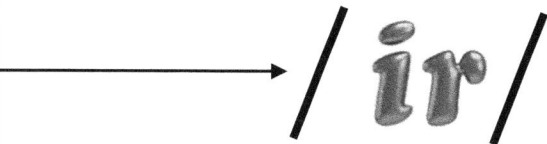

sk i r t

or	→	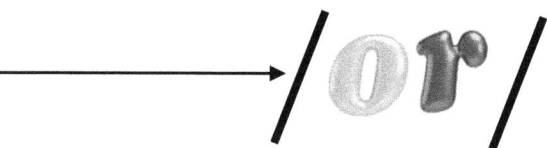

o r ange

ur	→	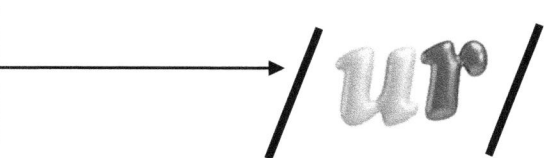

n u r se

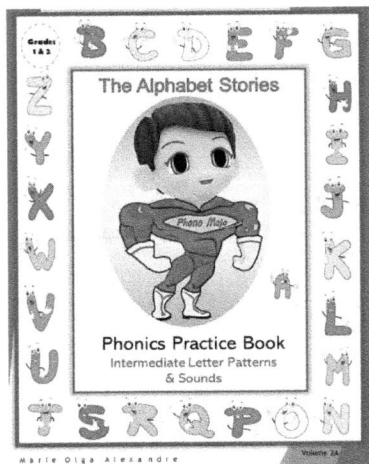

www.ingramcontent.com/pod-product-compliance
Lightning Source LLC
LaVergne TN
LVHW081348060426
835508LV00017B/1480